COUNTING

by Brenda Walpole
Illustrations by Dennis Tinkler
Photographs by Chris Fairclough

Contents

9 6 - 9900

Gareth Stevens Publishing
MILWAUKEE

How many?

Imagine how difficult life would be if you could not count. How would you tell the time or shop? How would you know how many days were left until your next birthday?

Sometimes we only need to know approximately "how many," and we don't need to count exactly. In this photograph, it's easy to see that there is more traffic on one side of the road than on the other side.

At other times, you need to count exactly. You need to count exactly to answer the question: "How many bales of hay are there in the field?" And when you take a test at school, your teacher needs to count precisely the number of questions you have answered correctly.

Counting is so important that numbers are some of the first words people learn to say. Many nursery rhymes are about counting. Do you remember the rhymes: "One, two, buckle my shoe," or "One, two, three, four, five, once I caught a fish alive?" For thousands of years, all over the world, children have sung counting rhymes. Can you think of any other rhymes or songs that are about counting?

3

Counting without writing

In prehistoric times, people probably used only a few counting words, such as *one*, *two*, and *many*. Because there were fewer people, they probably didn't need to know exactly how many, but only if there was enough.

When people began to live together in larger groups and to trade goods, they needed to count more accurately and keep records. People started to count using their fingers. But this didn't provide them with a way of recording numbers.

Probably one of the first ways of recording numbers was to use a tally stick. This was a bone or stick onto which lines or notches could be cut. Each line or notch stood for a unit. William Hogarth made this engraving in 1740 of a milkmaid holding out a tally stick for payment of the bill.

Something to try

Make your own tally sticks

You will need: cardboard, scissors, objects to count: e.g., marbles, thread spools, pencils.

Cut the cardboard into strips about 6 inches (15 centimeters) long. Try to show the amount in each group of objects by cutting notches in your cardboard tally sticks. You can cut different sizes of notches to represent different amounts. How many ways can you show the number of marbles you have? Can you think of a way to show a very large number on your tally sticks?

In the fourteenth century, the Inca people of South America recorded numbers by tying knots in a cord called a quipu. Each knot stood for one unit. A simple quipu had a series of identical knots tied on a single cord, but there were more complicated types of quipu. A large quipu was made from many single quipu cords. Different knots, such as single, double, or slip knots, stood for different amounts. The position of the knot on the cord was also important.

In every Inca settlement, there were four people referred to as "quipu keepers." They kept a note of the taxes owed to the government by recording the amounts on quipu cords.

Something to try

Make your own quipu

You will need: cord or string, scissors, objects to count.

Cut the cord or string into different lengths. To record a total number of objects, tie knots along the length of the cord. You may want to tie a double knot to record the number ten or twenty. See if the other children in your class can guess the number you have made on your quipu.

P.S. Try to make a quipu that shows the amount 125.

5

The first written numbers

There have been many different ways of writing amounts as number-signs. These signs are called numerals. We usually use the system that begins with the numerals 1, 2, 3, 4, 5. The earliest known written records of amounts are on clay tablets made by the Sumerians, who lived in Mesopotamia in about 3000 B.C. This tablet lists areas of fields and crops. The half-circle and circle marks on the tablet represent numbers. They were made by pressing the rounded end of the writing instrument into the clay.

The ancient Egyptian number system was more advanced than the Sumerian system. This was because the Egyptians were able to write their number-signs or numerals onto a type of early paper called papyrus. They used hieroglyphic signs to represent numerals. Straight lines were used to record the numerals one to nine. The numeral ten was a "hill" like this ∩, and the numeral one hundred was like this ℮. The symbol for one million was a man with his arms raised in surprise.

Look at the following examples of Egyptian numerals:

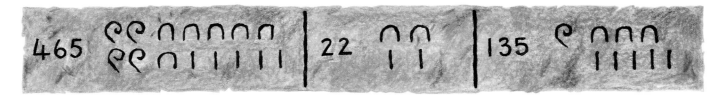

Can you translate this Egyptian numeral into the numerals we use today?

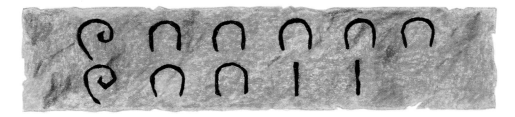

In ancient China, bamboo counting sticks called chou were used to record numerals. The sticks were arranged in patterns on a counting board. Look at the following Chinese numerals using chou:

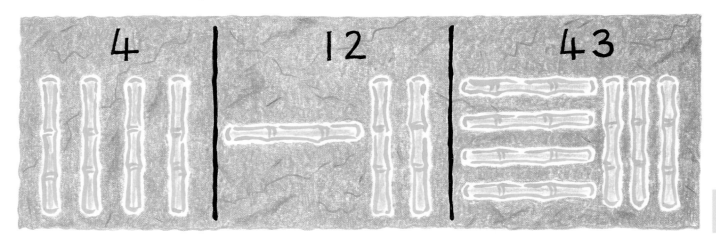

Writing large numbers

The ancient Egyptians and Chinese needed to write large numbers to help them study medicine, astronomy, science, and architecture. To avoid lining up hundreds of chou or drawing many lines of hieroglyphic signs, both the Egyptians and the Chinese invented new ways to show large numbers. This Egyptian papyrus from 1600 B.C. is called the Rhind-Ahmes Mathematical Papyrus.

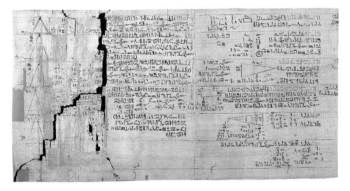

The Egyptians developed their hieroglyphics into a system called hieratics. Instead of writing rows of the "10" signs, , they invented an individual sign for each multiple of 10. For example, instead of writing ninety like this,

they used the sign

It was much quicker to use the hieratic system to write large numbers.

The Chinese invented new ways of arranging the chou sticks to record large numbers. They showed ninety like this:

Instead of using nine sticks lined up, they only needed to use five sticks.

Something to try

Invent your own number system

Try to make your own number system. You can experiment with dots and lines or shapes to represent different amounts. Think about ways of showing large numbers.

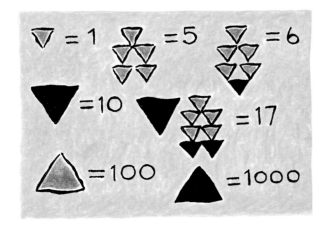

The Romans also had their own system of writing numbers. We can still see some Roman numerals in use today. Look for Roman numerals on clocks and on foundation stones of old buildings.

The Romans used seven signs to show numbers. You can see them in the table on the right.

Roman signs probably show the shapes made when counting on the fingers. The shapes of the numerals I, II, and III look like one, two, or three fingers being held up. The sign for five, V, looks like the hand being held with the thumb open. Put your hands back to back. Can you make the sign for ten? Any large number can be shown using combinations of the seven basic signs of the Roman system.

We often call an individual number a "digit." This word comes from the Latin word for finger. Latin was the language used by the Romans.

The Romans also thought of a way of making their written numbers shorter. Instead of writing VIIII for the number nine, they wrote IX, which means "ten less one." IX is much shorter than VIIII.

Roman numerals were used throughout Europe until medieval times. In monasteries, where monks were taught to read and write in Latin, no other way of counting was used. However, until the nineteenth century, most ordinary people still used tally sticks to count because they could not read or write.

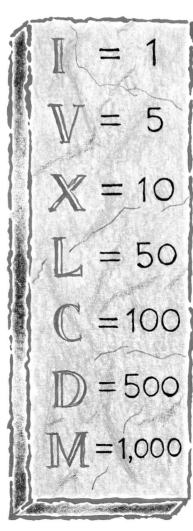

I = 1
V = 5
X = 10
L = 50
C = 100
D = 500
M = 1,000

Modern numbers

The numerals we use today are probably based on symbols used by Hindu mathematicians in India between 200 B.C. and A.D. 600. The use of these Hindu numerals spread through northern Africa and into Spain. These were lands where Arabic-speaking people lived. Because most Europeans learned about the numerals through Arabic-speaking people, we call these numerals "Arabic numerals."

Arabic numerals did not spread through Europe immediately. In the tenth century, most Europeans knew that Arab mathematicians used nine symbols and a "secret sign" or "zero," which meant they could write any number. But most people continued to do calculations on the abacus because they did not have paper or ink for writing. Most merchants and mathematicians began to use Arabic numerals after the appearance of a book by Leonardo Fibonacci in 1202. It was called *Liber Abaci,* which means "freedom from the abacus," and it explained how to use Arabic numerals. But it was not until about 1500 that all Europeans were familiar with Arabic numerals.

The illustration on the right shows our numerals and the numerals used by Arabic people today. Both number systems have developed from ancient Hindu numerals. Can you see any similarities between the two sets of numerals?

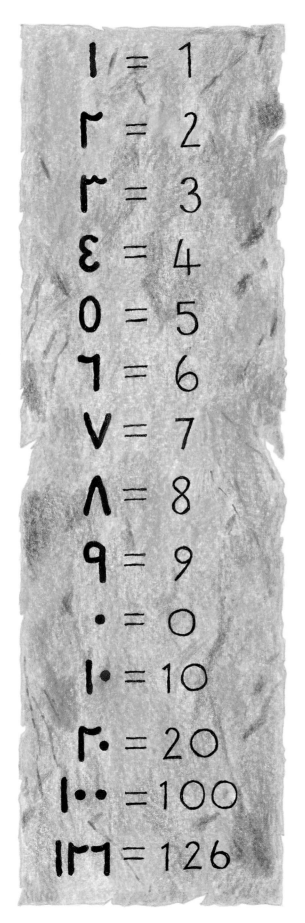

The Arabic system of writing numbers is quicker to use than the Roman system because the value of each number can be determined from its position. For example, in the number 523, we know there are 5 hundreds, 2 tens, and 3 ones.

The zero sign also makes writing very large numbers possible. In the United States, the numeral 1 followed by six zeros (1,000,000) is one million, which is the same as one thousand thousand in Britain. In the United States, a billion is one thousand million, and a trillion is a million million. In Great Britain, a billion is one million million, and a trillion is one million billion. Try to find out how some of these very big numbers would be written in Roman numerals.

The number 1,000,000,000,000 is either an American trillion or a British billion.

Something to try

Try translating the following Roman, Chinese, and Egyptian numerals into the numbers we use today. Which numeral is the easiest to explain to someone?

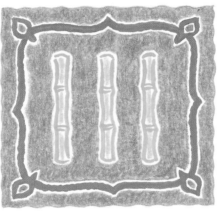

 P.S. What is today's date in Roman numerals?

Counting systems

In our system of counting, we work in groups, or sets, of ten. This is called the decimal system, from the Latin word *decem*, which means "ten." In Europe, people have been counting in sets of ten since the tenth century.

When using the metric system, you usually count to ten in one unit and then change to a bigger unit. There are ten millimeters in one centimeter and one hundred centimeters in one meter. When counting money, one hundred cents make one dollar. We also use sets, or groups, of numbers other than ten.

We use watches and clocks to tell time. There are sixty seconds in one minute and sixty minutes in one hour. How many hours are there in one day?

In computing and electronics, a counting system called the binary system is used. In the binary system, we count in sets of two. Only two symbols are used, 0 and 1. The *0* always means "zero." But the *1* does not always mean "one."

If a column has a 1 in it, another 1 cannot be added. The next column to the left must be used. A 1 in the first column to the right represents one, but after that the value of 1 doubles each time you move one column to the left.

0001 = 1	0100 = 4	0111 = 7
0010 = 2	0101 = 5	1000 = 8
0011 = 3	0110 = 6	1001 = 9

P.S. How would you write the number 10 in the binary system?

Countdown

To show that something is getting smaller, we can count backward. For example, as we get nearer a destination, the distance shown on the road signs gets smaller.

In which order would you see these road signs if you were driving to Chicago?

I 94 Chicago 15   **I 94 Chicago 90**   **I 94 Chicago 50**

Before a rocket is launched, there is a countdown. Minutes and seconds are counted backward as the rocket is checked. When zero is reached, the rocket is ready to be launched. This rocket has just reached blast-off.

If we count farther backward, past zero, numbers become negative integers, or minus numbers. On the Fahrenheit scale, after temperatures pass zero, minus numbers are eventually used to describe these very low temperatures; for example, - 5°F. Can you think of other times when you would need to use negative integers?

P.S. If the temperature is -22°F (-30°C) in Moscow and 86°F (30°C) in London, what is the difference in temperature between the two cities?

13

Tools for calculation

When people trade or share things with each other, they need to add, subtract, multiply, and divide numbers. This is called calculating.

Roman numbers are difficult to add and subtract, so the Romans calculated numbers on a counting board with pebbles. The word *calculation* comes from the Latin word *calculi*, which means "small stones." The counting board had three columns — one for ones, one for tens, and one for hundreds. When the ones column had ten pebbles in it, the ten pebbles were replaced by one single pebble in the tens column. When Roman citizens had to pay bills, they said they were "called to the pebbles."

Something to try

Make your own Roman counting board

You will need: modeling clay, marbles, a shoe box lid, a rolling pin.

Using the rolling pin, roll the clay into four long strips, about 3/4 inch (2 cm) wide and long enough to fit the length of the shoe box lid. The first strip is for the ones column, the second for the tens, the third for the hundreds, and the fourth for the thousands. Lay each strip in the lid, and make a groove along the length of each one with your finger to keep the marbles in place.

Try to record the number 372 on your counting board. Practice recording different numbers. Now try doing some calculations. Work out the answers to the following problems using your board: 67+189, 745+435, 278-103.

The Chinese abacus

For many centuries, people have used an abacus to figure out complicated calculations. Today, the abacus is still used in some parts of the world.

The Chinese abacus or *suan pan*, like the one in this photograph, has nine parallel dowels or wires with seven beads on each. The two top beads on each dowel are separated from the other five beads at the bottom by a middle bar. The beads are active only when they are moved to the middle bar.

To record a number, you must start by using the beads on the first dowel on the right side of the abacus. If you want to record the number 5, move all five beads up to the bar.

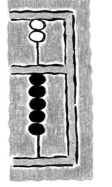

You can also record the number 5 by moving one bead from the top section down to the bar. The illustration on the right shows the two different ways of showing that one bead "down" from the top section of the abacus is worth five beads "up" from the bottom section.

When you have reached the number 10, the beads on the second dowel must be used. The beads on the second dowel stand for tens. Five beads "up" mean 50. Can you figure out the other way of showing 50 on the second dowel? When the number 100 is reached, the third dowel must be used. This abacus shows the number 365.

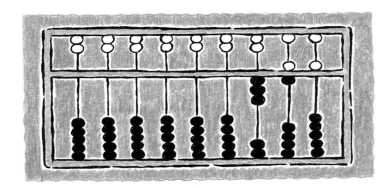

Where would you place the beads to show the number 2,704?

Napier's bones

In 1617, a Scottish mathematician named John Napier invented a set of calculating rods that helped make multiplication and division problems much easier to solve. The rods were often made from bone. This photograph shows a cylinder version of Napier's bones.

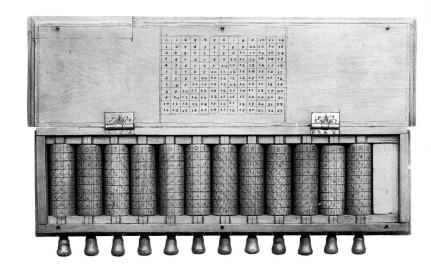

The rods work by changing difficult multiplication problems into simple addition problems. Each rod begins with a number from 0 to 9, and beneath that number is its multiplication table. To multiply two numbers together, for example 37 and 24, place the rods that show the numbers 3 and 7 next to each other as they are in the illustration on the right. This gives you 37 in the first row.

Then, multiply 37 by the number 4 by looking at the fourth row and adding the numbers in the columns diagonally, as shown below. You will get an answer of 148.

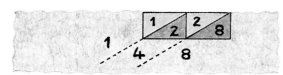

Next, you must multiply 37 by 20. You do this by multiplying by 2 and then adding a 0 to the answer. This is the same as multiplying by 20. To multiply 37 by 2, look at the second row and add the numbers in the columns diagonally. Then add a 0. You will get an answer of 740.

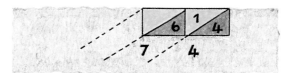

You can now find the result by adding these two numbers together, like this:

Make your own Napier's bones

You will need:
cardboard, a ruler, a pencil, a pen, a calculator.

Divide the cardboard into ten columns and then each column into nine squares. Divide the bottom eight squares with a diagonal line. You can see in the photograph below that the children have made rods for the numbers 1, 4, and 8. Try making your first rod for the number 7. Look at the illustration of a number 7 rod on the opposite page and fill in the numbers on your rod in the same way. Think of your seven times table. What do you notice about the numbers you have just filled in? All the rods work in the same way. Can you make a rod for the number 6? Try doing different multiplication problems using your rods. Check your answers on a calculator.

P.S. Did you know Napier also invented logarithms? Until about twenty years ago, they were used for multiplication. Can you find out what they are?

17

Mechanical calculating tools

In 1642, a French mathematician named Blaise Pascal invented the first working calculator. It was a mechanical instrument, which means it worked without electricity. Inside, it had several gear wheels with numbers marked on the rims. Numbers to be added or subtracted were dialed in and appeared in the window at the top.

More than two hundred years later, in 1892, William Burroughs built the first adding and subtracting machine that could print out an answer.

Burroughs's adding machines, like the one shown in this photograph, were used in banks and offices until the 1960s. The operator pressed the keys on top of the machine and then turned the handle to calculate the answer. The result was printed on the roll of paper. Later, electricity was used instead of the mechanical handle to make the machine work.

Charles Babbage, who lived from 1791-1871, is often called "the father of the modern computer." Babbage designed a machine that he called an "analytical engine." His engine was designed to perform any calculation. Instructions were to be put into the machine using punched cards. The engine had a memory unit to store numbers. Unfortunately, Babbage was never able to build his machine because it was too difficult for the engineers of that time to make. Babbage's calculating machine has now been built, using his original design. This photograph shows how complicated it is.

Modern calculating machines are electronic. They no longer use mechanical wheel movement to do calculations.

Number patterns

Since the time of the ancient Greeks, mathematicians have spent many hours searching for prime numbers. Any number that can only be divided by itself and the number 1 is called a prime number. The numbers 2, 3, and 5 are all prime numbers. But the number 6 is an example of a number that isn't a prime number, because it can be divided by the numbers 2 and 3 as well as 1 and 6.

Pythagoras, a Greek mathematician who lived between 560 B.C. and 480 B.C., was very interested in square numbers. The square of a number is the amount made when it is multiplied by itself. These square numbers are written like this: 2^2, 3^2, and so on.

2^2 means $2 \times 2 = 4$. 3^2 means $3 \times 3 = 9$.

Or they can be drawn as square patterns like this:

Can you figure out what 4^2 means? Can you draw it as a square pattern?

Magic squares

The first magic squares were probably made by the Chinese as long ago as 2800 B.C.

This is a 3 x 3 magic square, because it has three squares across and three squares down. Each number, from 1 to 9, is used only once. If you add up the numbers in the rows across, down, or diagonally, you will find that each row adds up to 15. This magic square is the only one that can be made from a 3 x 3 square.

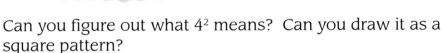

6	7	2
1	5	9
8	3	4

This photo shows a detail of an engraving by the German artist Albrecht Dürer. It contains a 4 x 4 magic square. In Dürer's magic square, each row across adds up to 34, as do the two diagonal rows and each of the four numbers in the corners. Can you find the date of the painting, 1514, within the magic square?

Make your own magic squares

There are 880 different ways of making a 4 x 4 magic square. See how many you can find.

You will need: 16 squares of cardboard, a pencil, paper, a calculator.

Number your squares of cardboard from 1 to 16. Lay them down in rows of four squares. Move the numbered squares around, keeping four squares in each row, until you have found a magic square. Check that the numbers in each row across, each row down, and each diagonal row add up to 34. On the graph paper, write down the pattern of any 4 x 4 magic squares you find.

P.S. There are more than 13 million different ways of making a 5 x 5 magic square in which each row adds up to 65.

Ratios

A ratio is a pair of numbers that can tell us how large one thing is when compared with another.

Sometimes ratios can be found in the instructions on labels and in cooking recipes. You can see a label from a bottle of orange concentrate on the right. It tells you to mix one part orange concentrate with three parts water. You mix the orange and the water in the ratio of one to three. This can be written by the numbers 1:3. If you change the ratio of concentrate to water, the drink will taste stronger or weaker.

To make perfect orange juice, mix one part concentrate to three parts water. For a delicious summer drink, add ice and a slice of orange.

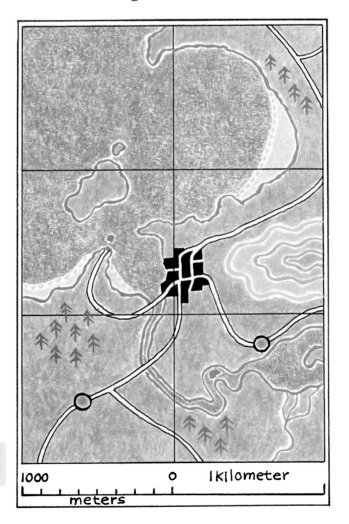

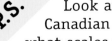

1000   0   1 kilometer

meters

If you look at a map, you will find a scale written as a ratio. On this European map with a metric scale, the ratio is 1:25,000. This means that 1 centimeter on the map represents 25,000 centimeters (or 250 m) on the ground. Measure the kilometer on the scale with a ruler. You will find that it is 4 centimeters long. This length represents 4 x 250 meters, which equals 1,000 meters, or one kilometer.

Some maps show more detail than others, depending on the scales they use. You can see more detail on a map with a scale of 1:2,000 (1 cm to 2,000 cm, or 20 m) than on a map with a scale of 1:10,000 (1 cm to 10,000 cm, or 100 m). Each centimeter on the first map would represent a smaller distance on the ground, and so could show more detail.

P.S. Look at some U.S. and Canadian maps and see what scales they use.

The ancient Greeks discovered a special ratio, called the "golden ratio," which they used to draw rectangles. The sides of the rectangles were in the ratio of 1:1.618. If, for example, one side was 1 yard long, the other side would be 1.618 yards long. The rectangles could be any size as long as the lengths of the sides were in these proportions. They were called "golden rectangles." These ratios were often included in buildings to make them look balanced and attractive.
In Athens, the Parthenon has a golden rectangle shape.

Golden rectangles can also be found in sizes we use today. Paper sizes, for example, are sometimes golden rectangles.

In the Middle Ages in Europe, artists and architects used the golden rectangle. They called it the "divine proportion." The Italian artist Leonardo da Vinci painted a famous picture of an old man. Find a copy of this painting in a book and look for the golden rectangles he painted over the man's face.

Numbers in nature

In 1202, Leonardo Fibonacci, an Italian mathematician, wrote about a special sequence of numbers in his book, *Liber Abaci*. This sequence is called the Fibonacci Sequence, and it runs like this:

1 1 2 3 5 8 13 21 34 55 89 144 . . . and so on.

Each number in the sequence is found by adding together the two numbers directly before it.

The Fibonacci Sequence is fascinating because it can be found in unexpected places in nature.

Something to try

Find your own Fibonacci numbers

You will need: a pineapple or a pinecone; flowers, such as an English daisy, a buttercup, and a forget-me-not; a marker.

Look carefully at the pineapple knobs. You will see that the knobs form two sets of spirals that go up the pineapple. Use a marker to make a mark on one knob at the bottom of the pineapple. The knob will be the first knob in a spiral. Does the spiral go clockwise or counter-clockwise? You will find eight spirals that go up around the pineapple clockwise and thirteen that go counter-clockwise. The numbers 8 and 13 can be found next to each other in the Fibonacci Sequence. You can try the same investigation with a pinecone.

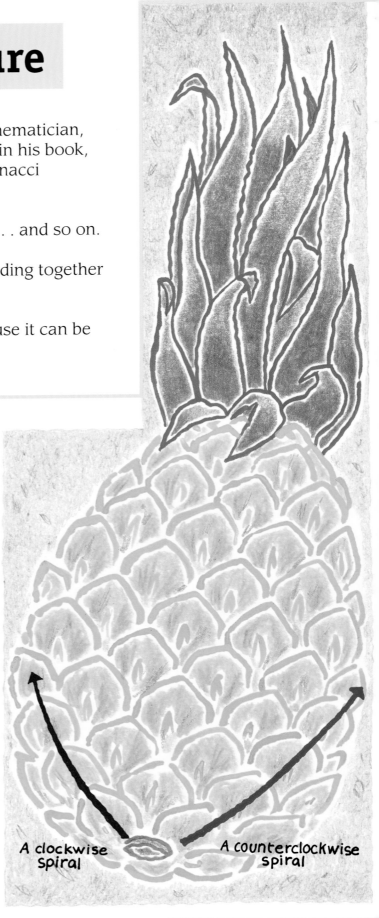

A clockwise spiral

A counterclockwise spiral

Fibonacci flowers

Another place to look for Fibonacci numbers is in a garden or a park. If you count the petals of certain flowers, you will find that the total number of petals often adds up to a number or a series of numbers in the Fibonacci Sequence. Buttercups and forget-me-nots always have five petals. An English daisy's petals are arranged in three rings. The inside ring has thirty-four petals, the middle ring fifty-five petals, and the outer ring eighty-nine — three numbers in the sequence.

Other flowers have a total number of petals that add up to a number in the Fibonacci Sequence. Try counting the petals of various other flowers. Which numbers can you find?

This turtle has thirteen plates on the main part of its shell. If you see a tortoise or a turtle in a zoo or in a pet shop, count the total number of sections on the main part of its shell. How many are there? It is always the same number.

P.S. Choose a series of three numbers from any part of the Fibonacci Sequence; for example, 5, 8, 13. Take the first number and multiply it by the third number (5 x 13 = 65). Take the middle number and multiply it by itself (8 x 8 = 64). Subtract the second answer from the first answer. The final answer is always 1!

Plotting numbers

On a graph, we can use numbers to "plot" certain points that we can then join to make lines or shapes.

To plot the point (1, 2) on this graph, you would move one square along the horizontal line and two squares up the vertical line.

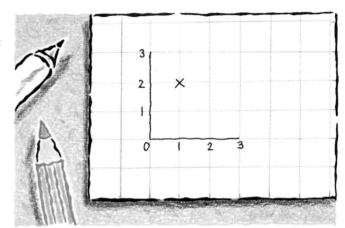

Something to try

Discover the hidden letter

You will need:
graph paper, a pencil, a ruler.

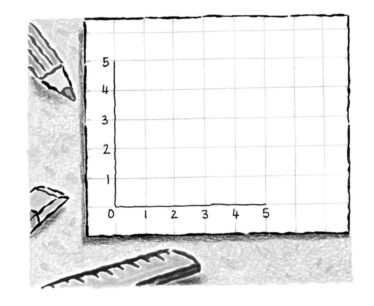

Copy the vertical and horizontal lines shown here and label them with the numbers 1 to 5. Now plot these points:

(1,1)   (1,5)   (3,3)   (5,5)   (5,1).

Using a ruler, connect the points in the order given. What have you made?

We can also use numbers to locate a certain building or town on a map. To do this, we use the reference number given for that town or building. A map reference number is written using a number and a letter; for example, B3. The map is divided into equal squares. On the horizontal line, each square is labeled by a letter, and on the vertical line, each square is labeled by a number.

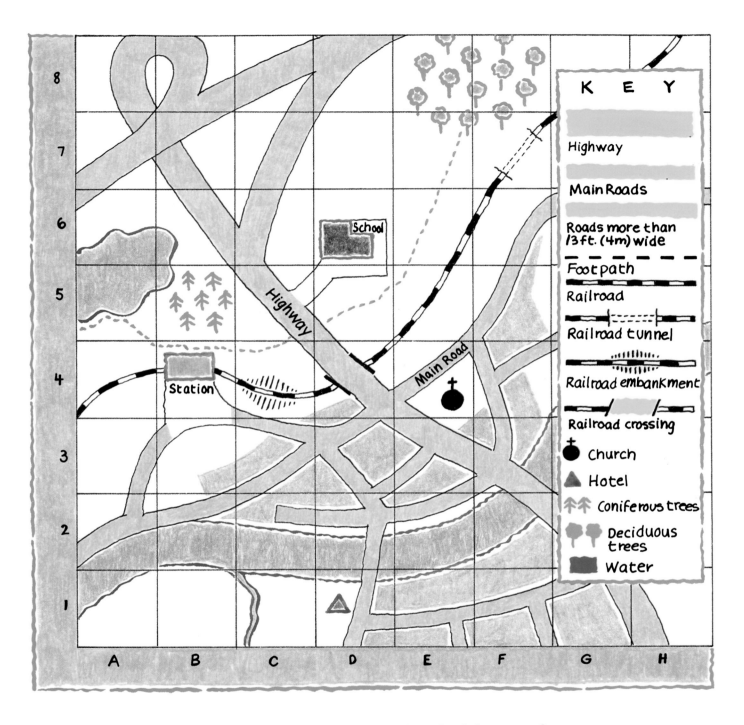

Look at this map. To find the church, which has a reference number of E4, place one finger on the letter E and another on the number 4. Slide your fingers along these lines until they meet in the square E4. You will find the church in this square. What can you find at the following references?

B5   D1   F7

What are the reference numbers for the school and for the railroad station?

How calculating has changed

Since the days of tally sticks and counting boards, calculating machines have come a long way. Today, most of us use a pocket calculator to do our calculations. This tiny machine can give an answer to a difficult problem in seconds. Imagine how long it would take to do these calculations using a Roman counting board or even Pascal's calculator: 121+17, 78-23, 273 x 14.
See how quickly you can find the answers using a pocket calculator.

Today, most people keep their money in bank accounts. With a special code number, they can take money out of their accounts from cash machines sometimes called automatic tellers. These machines are linked to the bank's computer, which can calculate how much money their customers have in their accounts. The computer can also print out statements and receipts. Statements show a record of each time money has been deposited into or withdrawn from the account. People no longer need to keep these records on tally sticks or quipus.

This modern checkout machine uses a scanner to read a series of numbers, shown in the form of a bar code, on each item. From its memory, the machine can print out the price of each item on the register receipt and add the prices together as each item passes the scanner. If a series of these machines is linked to the store's computer, the total number of each item sold can be recorded. The manager can then know when it is time to reorder certain products.

Modern computers are powerful machines that can work very quickly to give answers to very complicated calculations. Information can be put into the computer from a keyboard, and answers can be printed on paper, shown on a screen, or even produced as a voice. You probably have a computer in your classroom or at home. Some computers are smaller than a briefcase.

Important events

3000 B.C. — The Sumerians were using one of the first known number systems. Amounts were recorded by carving marks on clay tablets.

2800 B.C. — The first magic squares were thought to have been drawn by Chinese mathematicians.

1600 B.C. — The ancient Egyptians wrote mathematical problems on the Rhind-Ahmes Papyrus.

200 B.C.–A.D. 600 — Hindu mathematicians developed numbers on which our present-day numbers are probably based.

1200 — The British Exchequer used tally sticks to record tax payments.

1202 — Leonardo Fibonacci published a book on Arabic numerals titled *Liber Abaci*.

1600 — Writing fractions as decimals began in Europe.

1617 — John Napier invented "Napier's bones" to speed up multiplication.

1642 — Blaise Pascal, a French mathematician, invented a calculator.

1835 — Charles Babbage designed his "analytical engine," a forerunner of the modern computer.

1852 — The highest number named in the dictionary, the googol (the number 1 followed by six hundred zeroes), was first recorded.

1892 — William Burroughs built the first adding machine that could print out an answer.

1940 — The first electrically operated computers were built.

1975 — The first personal computer was available for purchase.

1980 — The first portable computers, or laptops, were manufactured.

1988 — Notebook computers, even smaller than laptops, became popular.

For more information

More things to do

1. The Fibonacci Sequence runs like this:
   1   1   2   3   5   8   13   21   34
   55   89   144   233 . . . and so on.
   Divide each number in the sequence by the number in front of it. Use a calculator to help you. You will find that you get a series of decimals like this: 1, 2, 1.5, 1.67, and so on. As you go farther along the sequence, the decimals will get closer and closer to 1.618, which is part of the golden ratio 1:618. (See page 23).

2. Learn about the Braille system, which uses raised dots to represent numbers and letters. This system was devised by Frenchman Louis Braille in 1829. What configuration of dots is used to represent the number 7? The number 3? Can you find any places where Braille symbols are used to represent numbers?

3. There are many sayings about numbers: See if you can find out what these mean: "pieces of eight," "at sixes and sevens," "in two minds," "back to square one." How many more sayings can you think of or find?

4. When we write addresses, we usually add a zip code so our letters can be sorted by machine. In the United States, every state and every town has its own code number. The first two numbers in a zip code represent the code for the state, and the last three numbers represent the code for the town. The code for the state of Illinois is 60, and the code for the town of Elk Grove is 007, so a letter going to this town should have 60007 written on it. Find the codes for the states of California, Louisiana, Minnesota, North Carolina, and your state if it is not one of these.

More books to read

How Did We Find Out About Numbers? Isaac Asimov (Walker)
Mathematics. Irving Adler (Doubleday)
Number Patterns. Marion Smoothey (Marshall Cavendish)
Numbers. Philip Carona (Childrens Press)
Numbers. Henry A. Pluckrose (Franklin Watts)
Numbers. Marion Smoothey (Marshall Cavendish)
The Science Book of Numbers. Jack Challoner (Harcourt, Brace, Jovanovich)

Videotapes

In Search of the Missing Numbers. (Davidson Videos)
Math Rock Countdown. (Davidson Videos)
Place Values: Ones, Tens, Hundreds. (Coronet)

Places to visit

Goudreau Museum of Mathematics
Herricks Community Center
999 Herricks Road, Room 202
New Hyde Park, NY 11040-1302

National Museum of Science
  and Technology
1867 Saint Laurent Boulevard
Ottawa, Ontario K1G 5A3

Computer Museum
300 Congress Street
Museum Wharf
Boston, MA 02210

Science World
1455 Quebec Street
Vancouver, British Columbia
V6A 3Z7

Index

For a free color catalog describing Gareth Stevens' list of high-quality books, call 1-800-542-2595 (USA) or 1-800-461-9120 (Canada). Gareth Stevens' Fax: (414) 225-0377.

Library of Congress Cataloging-in-Publication Data available upon request from publisher. Fax: (414) 225-0377 for the attention of the Publishing Records Department.

ISBN 0-8368-1359-6

This edition first published in 1995 by **Gareth Stevens Publishing** 1555 North RiverCenter Drive, Suite 201 Milwaukee, Wisconsin 53212, USA

This edition © 1995 by Gareth Stevens, Inc. Original edition published in 1995 by A & C Black (Publishers) Ltd., 35 Bedford Row, London WC1R 4JH. © 1995 A & C Black (Publishers) Ltd. Additional end matter © 1995 by Gareth Stevens, Inc.

Acknowledgements
Photographs by Chris Fairclough, except for: p. 2 Lifefile Photo Agency; p. 4 Ann Ronan Picture Library; p. 5 Mary Evans Picture Library; pp. 6, 8, 9, 15, 18 Michael Holford; p. 13 NASA/Science Photo Library; pp. 16, 19 Science Museum Library; p. 21 Albrecht Dürer's Melancholia (detail), Bridgeman Art Library; p. 23 Spectrum Color Library; p. 28 Barclays Bank PLC; p. 29 (t) Picture of a "Check-A-Bag" unit at Safeway's checkout by courtesy of LINPAC Plastics International Ltd.; p. 29 (b) Apple Computer UK Limited.

Printed in Mexico
1 2 3 4 5 6 7 8 9 99 98 97 96 95